TREE FINDER

A Manual for the Identification of Trees by Their Leaves

May Theilgaard Watts

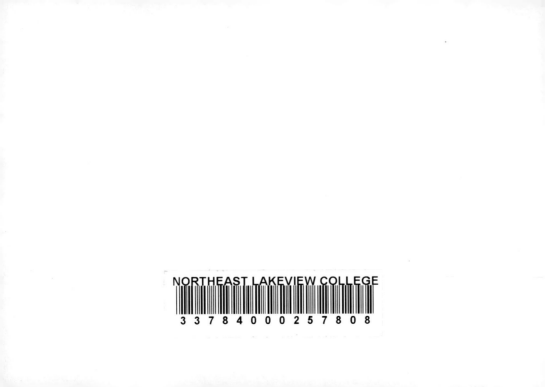

TREE FINDER

A Manual for the Identification
of Trees by Their Leaves

by **May Theilgaard Watts**

NATURE STUDY GUILD PUBLISHERS
A division of Keen Communications, Birmingham, AL
keencommunication.com

T O   U S E   T H I S   K E Y

1. Select a typical leaf from the tree you wish to identify. Avoid freaks.

2. Start at the top of Page 5 or

3. Proceed step by step, considering both choices under each symbol or

4. When you have made the final choice, arriving at the name of the leaf, compare your leaf with the illustration, and check the other features shown.

advice: examine pages 1, 2, 3, and 4, before starting on page 5

THE DISTRIBUTION OF NATIVE TREES

he areas shown on the small green maps beside the trees are those in which the tree grows wild. Some of these res are planted by people over a much wider area.

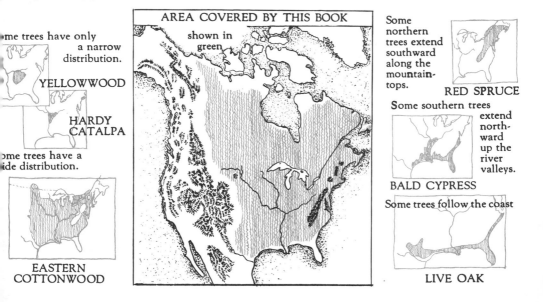

me trees have only a narrow distribution.

YELLOWWOOD

HARDY CATALPA

me trees have a ide distribution.

EASTERN COTTONWOOD

AREA COVERED BY THIS BOOK

shown in green

Some northern trees extend southward along the mountain-tops.

RED SPRUCE

Some southern trees extend north-ward up the river valleys.

BALD CYPRESS

Some trees follow the coast

LIVE OAK

the HABITAT of a tree, the place where it is likely to grow naturally,
is indicated beside the leaf of each NATIVE TREE

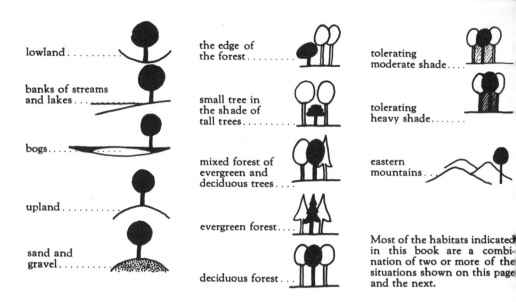

lowland..........

banks of streams
and lakes.....

bogs.....

upland..........

sand and
gravel..........

the edge of
the forest..........

small tree in
the shade of
tall trees..........

mixed forest of
evergreen and
deciduous trees....

evergreen forest....

deciduous forest...

tolerating
moderate shade....

tolerating
heavy shade.......

eastern
mountains...

Most of the habitats indicated
in this book are a combi-
nation of two or more of the
situations shown on this page
and the next.

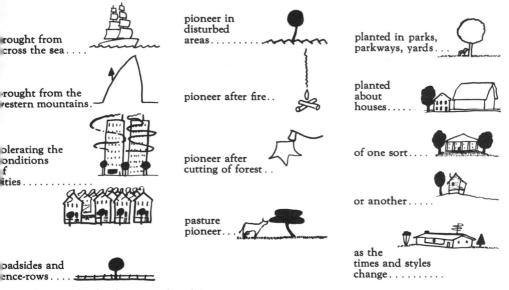

brought from
across the sea....

brought from the
western mountains.

tolerating the
conditions
of
cities............

roadsides and
fence-rows....

pioneer in
disturbed
areas.........

pioneer after fire..

pioneer after
cutting of forest..

pasture
pioneer...

planted in parks,
parkways, yards...

planted
about
houses......

of one sort....

or another.....

as the
times and styles
change.........

the same kinds of trees are found in
fence-rows, pastures, and the edge of the forest.

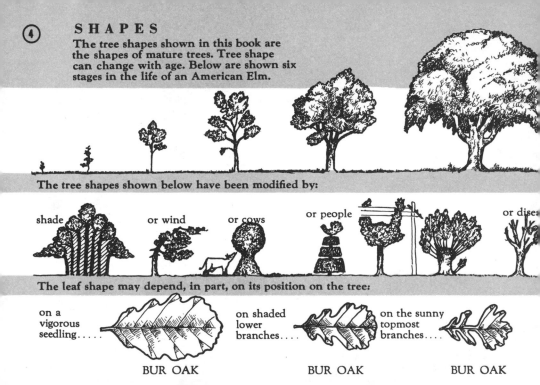

④ **SHAPES**

The tree shapes shown in this book are the shapes of mature trees. Tree shape can change with age. Below are shown six stages in the life of an American Elm.

The tree shapes shown below have been modified by:

shade   or wind   or cows   or people   or disease

The leaf shape may depend, in part, on its position on the tree:

on a vigorous seedling.....   on shaded lower branches....   on the sunny topmost branches....

BUR OAK   BUR OAK   BUR OAK

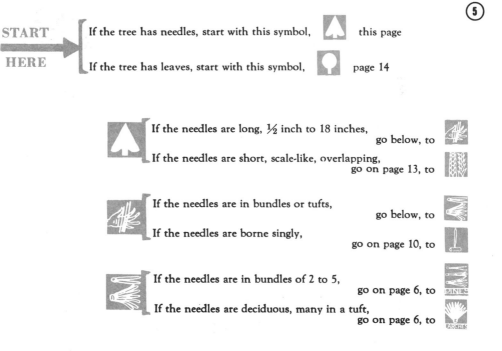

START HERE

If the tree has needles, start with this symbol, this page

If the tree has leaves, start with this symbol, page 14

If the needles are long, ½ inch to 18 inches, go below, to

If the needles are short, scale-like, overlapping, go on page 13, to

If the needles are in bundles or tufts, go below, to

If the needles are borne singly, go on page 10, to

If the needles are in bundles of 2 to 5, go on page 6, to

If the needles are deciduous, many in a tuft, go on page 6, to

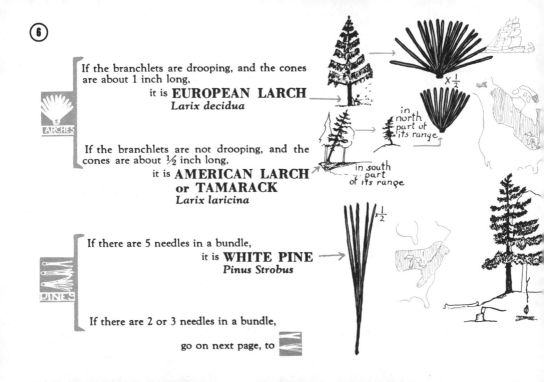

If the branchlets are drooping, and the cones are about 1 inch long,

it is **EUROPEAN LARCH**
Larix decidua

If the branchlets are not drooping, and the cones are about ½ inch long,

it is **AMERICAN LARCH**
or TAMARACK
Larix laricina

in north part of its range

in south part of its range

LARCHES

If there are 5 needles in a bundle,

it is **WHITE PINE**
Pinus Strobus

If there are 2 or 3 needles in a bundle,

go on next page, to

PINES

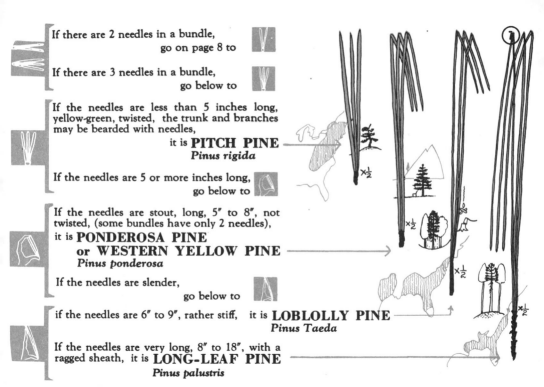

If there are 2 needles in a bundle, go on page 8 to

If there are 3 needles in a bundle, go below to

If the needles are less than 5 inches long, yellow-green, twisted, the trunk and branches may be bearded with needles, it is **PITCH PINE**
Pinus rigida

If the needles are 5 or more inches long, go below to

If the needles are stout, long, 5″ to 8″, not twisted, (some bundles have only 2 needles), it is **PONDEROSA PINE** **or WESTERN YELLOW PINE** →
Pinus ponderosa

If the needles are slender, go below to

if the needles are 6″ to 9″, rather stiff, it is **LOBLOLLY PINE** →
Pinus Taeda

If the needles are very long, 8″ to 18″, with a ragged sheath, it is **LONG-LEAF PINE** →
Pinus palustris

(8)

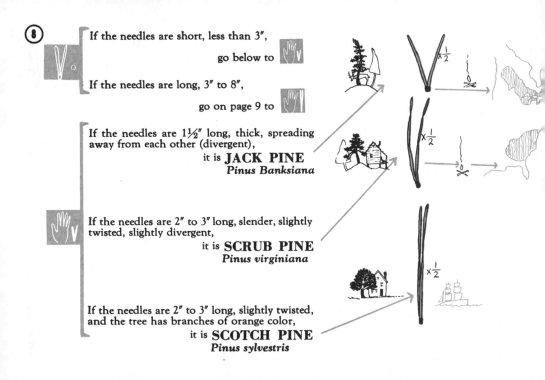

If the needles are short, less than 3″,

go below to

If the needles are long, 3″ to 8″,

go on page 9 to

If the needles are 1½″ long, thick, spreading away from each other (divergent),

it is **JACK PINE**
Pinus Banksiana

If the needles are 2″ to 3″ long, slender, slightly twisted, slightly divergent,

it is **SCRUB PINE**
Pinus virginiana

If the needles are 2″ to 3″ long, slightly twisted, and the tree has branches of orange color,

it is **SCOTCH PINE**
Pinus sylvestris

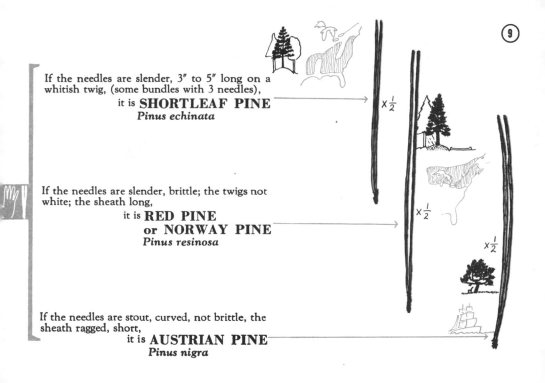

If the needles are slender, 3″ to 5″ long on a whitish twig, (some bundles with 3 needles),

it is **SHORTLEAF PINE**
Pinus echinata

x ½

If the needles are slender, brittle; the twigs not white; the sheath long,

it is **RED PINE**
or NORWAY PINE
Pinus resinosa

x ½

x ½

If the needles are stout, curved, not brittle, the sheath ragged, short,

it is **AUSTRIAN PINE**
Pinus nigra

If the needles are stiff, sharp, 4-sided, (can be twirled between the thumb and finger), and leave the twig rough when they fall off,

go below to

If the needles are flat and pliable,

go on page 12 to

If the needles are *extremely sharp,* and the branches form a flat, horizontal spray,

it is **COLORADO SPRUCE** ——→
Picea pungens

If the needles are not very sharp, nor the branches noticeably horizontal,

go below to

If the branchlets droop, and the cones are 4″ to 6″ long,

it is **NORWAY SPRUCE** ——→
Picea Abies

If the branchlets do not droop, and the cones are shorter,

go on next page, to

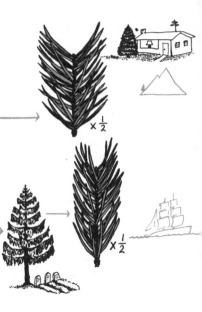

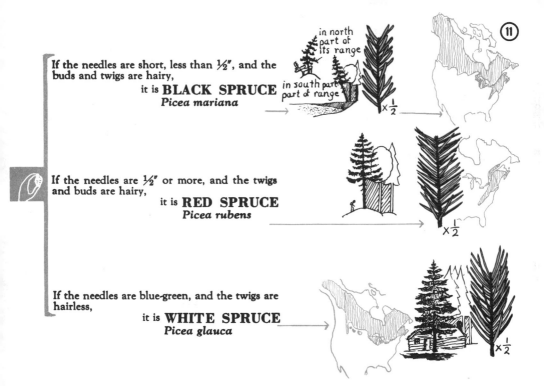

If the needles are short, less than ½", and the buds and twigs are hairy,

it is **BLACK SPRUCE**
Picea mariana

in north part of its range

in south part part of range

×½

If the needles are ½" or more, and the twigs and buds are hairy,

it is **RED SPRUCE**
Picea rubens

×½

If the needles are blue-green, and the twigs are hairless,

it is **WHITE SPRUCE**
Picea glauca

×½

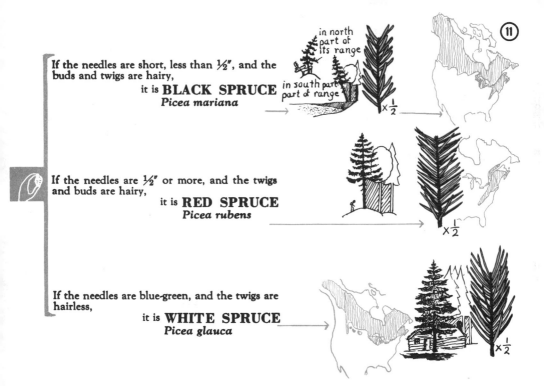

(12)

If the needles are 2-ranked, (like hair divided by a comb), go below to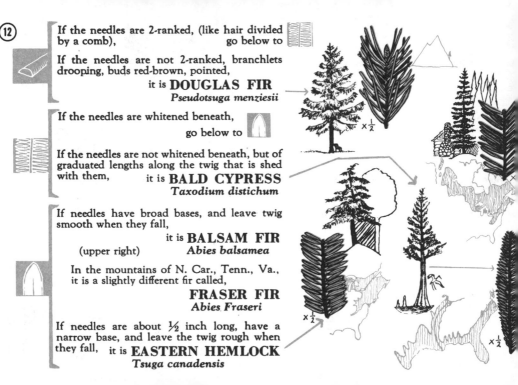

If the needles are not 2-ranked, branchlets drooping, buds red-brown, pointed,

it is **DOUGLAS FIR**
Pseudotsuga menziesii

If the needles are whitened beneath,
go below to

If the needles are not whitened beneath, but of graduated lengths along the twig that is shed with them, it is **BALD CYPRESS**
Taxodium distichum

If needles have broad bases, and leave twig smooth when they fall,

it is **BALSAM FIR**
(upper right) *Abies balsamea*

In the mountains of N. Car., Tenn., Va., it is a slightly different fir called,

FRASER FIR
Abies Fraseri

If needles are about ½ inch long, have a narrow base, and leave the twig rough when they fall, it is **EASTERN HEMLOCK**
Tsuga canadensis

If all the needles are scale-like

go below to

If part of the needles are small and scale-like and part are sharp and prickly,

it is RED CEDAR
Juniperus virginiana

If the needles are flat, forming a flattened spray; and if there are numerous ½″ cones; and the tree is in a swampy or limestone area,

it is ARBOR VITAE
Thuja occidentalis

If the needles are narrow scales, not in flat sprays, and if the numerous ¼″ to ½″ cones are globular, and if the tree is in a coastal swamp,

it is ATLANTIC WHITE CEDAR
Chamaecyparis thyoides

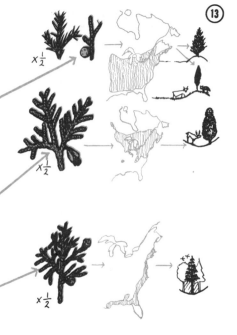

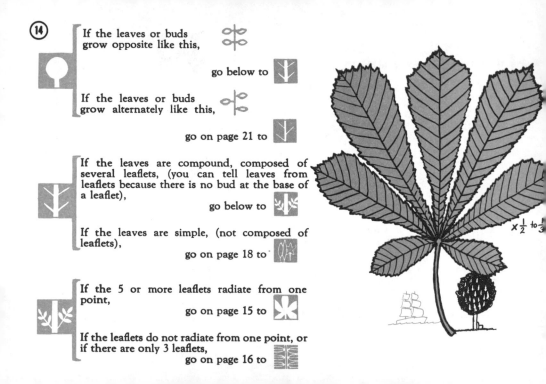

(14)

If the leaves or buds grow opposite like this,

go below to ↓

If the leaves or buds grow alternately like this,

go on page 21 to

If the leaves are compound, composed of several leaflets, (you can tell leaves from leaflets because there is no bud at the base of a leaflet),

go below to

If the leaves are simple, (not composed of leaflets),

go on page 18 to

If the 5 or more leaflets radiate from one point,

go on page 15 to

If the leaflets do not radiate from one point, or if there are only 3 leaflets,

go on page 16 to

$\times \frac{1}{2}$ to $\frac{1}{3}$

If there are usually 5 leaflets and each leaflet has a short stalk, and the winter buds are not sticky, go below to

If there are usually 7 leaflets, doubly-toothed, and the leaflets have no stalks, and the winter buds are sticky,

it is **HORSE CHESTNUT**
Aesculus Hippocastanum
See illustration on page 14

If the leaflets are irregularly and bluntly toothed, and the end buds are keeled, and the twigs have a disagreeable smell when bruised,

it is **OHIO BUCKEYE** ———→
Aesculus glabra

If the leaflets are regularly and finely toothed and the end buds are not keeled,
it is

SWEET BUCKEYE
YELLOW BUCKEYE
Aesculus octandra

× ½

× ½

× ½

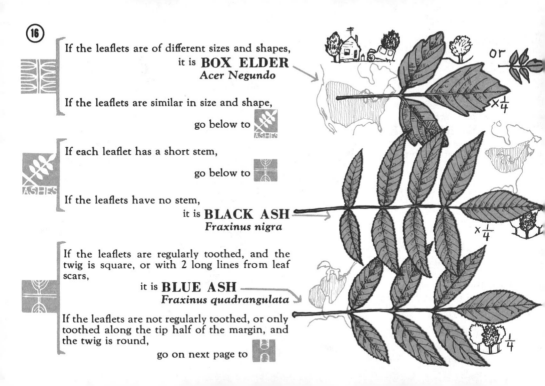

If the leaflets are of different sizes and shapes,
it is **BOX ELDER**
Acer Negundo

If the leaflets are similar in size and shape,

go below to

If each leaflet has a short stem,

go below to

If the leaflets have no stem,

it is **BLACK ASH**
Fraxinus nigra

If the leaflets are regularly toothed, and the twig is square, or with 2 long lines from leaf scars,

it is **BLUE ASH**
Fraxinus quadrangulata

If the leaflets are not regularly toothed, or only toothed along the tip half of the margin, and the twig is round,

go on next page to

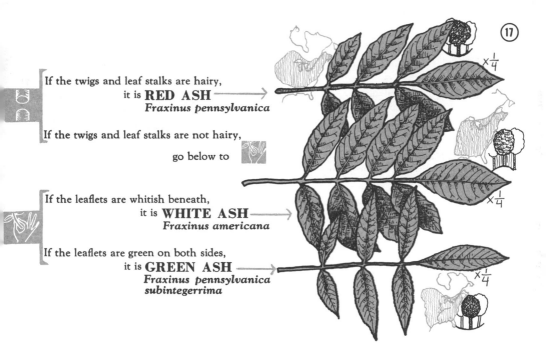

⑰

If the twigs and leaf stalks are hairy,
  it is **RED ASH** ⟶
    Fraxinus pennsylvanica

If the twigs and leaf stalks are not hairy,

    go below to

If the leaflets are whitish beneath,
  it is **WHITE ASH** ⟶
    Fraxinus americana

If the leaflets are green on both sides,
  it is **GREEN ASH** ⟶
    Fraxinus pennsylvanica
    subintegerrima

×¼

×¼

×¼

If each leaf has a single main vein with smaller side veins, and is without teeth or lobes,

go on page 21 to

If each leaf has 3 to 7 main veins radiating from one point, and is lobed,

go below to

If the notches between the lobes are V shaped, (either a broad or narrow V),

go below to

If the notches are U shaped,

go on page 20 to

If the leaves are distinctly 5-lobed,

go on page 19 to

If the leaves appear 3-lobed rather than 5-lobed, (the 2 basal lobes being small or absent),

go on page 19 to

$\times \frac{1}{2}$

If the leaf is rough-textured with an intricate network of veins, and is not white-downy beneath,

it is SYCAMORE MAPLE
Acer Pseudo-Platanus

picture on page 18

If the end lobe narrows toward its base, and the notches between the lobes are deep, and the under-surface is white-downy,

it is SILVER MAPLE
Acer saccharinum

If the leaf surface is rough with a network of depressed veins, and the lobes are drawn out to long tapering tips, and the teeth are all of somewhat the same size, and the tree is small, shrubby,

go on page 20 to

If the leaf surface is smooth, and the teeth of irregular sizes, and it is not a shrub,

it is RED MAPLE
Acer rubrum

over most of its range

on the prairie edge, and northeast

×½

×½

If leaves are finely-toothed, hairless; bark green with white stripes, it is

STRIPED MAPLE
Acer pensylvanicum
(upper right)

If leaves are coarsely toothed, and white-hairy beneath with hairy twigs, it is

MOUNTAIN MAPLE
Acer spicatum (upper left)

If leaf stem shows a milky juice when broken; leaf usually wider than long; base of leaf not curving,

it is **NORWAY MAPLE**
Acer platanoides (lower left)

If there is no milky juice; leaf about as long as wide; base of leaf curving, it is

SUGAR MAPLE
Acer saccharum (lower right)

(A similar tree, but with leaves hairy beneath, 3 lobed, with sides drooping, is
BLACK MAPLE
Acer nigrum)

$\times \frac{1}{2}$

$\times \frac{1}{2}$

$\times \frac{1}{2}$

$\times \frac{1}{2}$

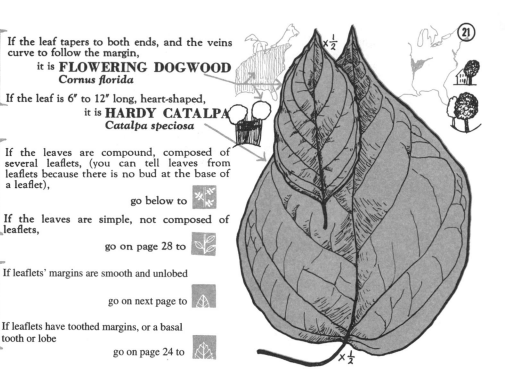

If the leaf tapers to both ends, and the veins curve to follow the margin,

it is **FLOWERING DOGWOOD**
Cornus florida

If the leaf is 6″ to 12″ long, heart-shaped,

it is **HARDY CATALPA**
Catalpa speciosa

If the leaves are compound, composed of several leaflets, (you can tell leaves from leaflets because there is no bud at the base of a leaflet),

go below to

If the leaves are simple, not composed of leaflets,

go on page 28 to

If leaflets' margins are smooth and unlobed

go on next page to

If leaflets have toothed margins, or a basal tooth or lobe

go on page 24 to

×½

×½

If tree is small, growing in a bog or ditch; leaflets more than an inch long, tapering to a V shape at both ends, (it may have drooping clusters of white berries.) Don't touch it!

it is **POISON SUMAC**
Toxicodendron vernix

If the tree is not in a swamp or bog, and the leaflets, or most of them, are rounded at one end or both, (the tree may have pea-like pods)

go below to

If the leaves, or some of them, are doubly compound, dividing and subdividing,

go on next page to

If the leaves are singly-compound,

go below to

If leaf tips are pointed,
it is **YELLOWWOOD** (center)
Cladrastus kentukea

If leaf tips are rounded; twigs have short, paired thorns, it is **BLACK LOCUST**
Robinia Pseudo-Acacia

If the leaflets are less than 1½″ long,

go below to

If the leaflets are 2″ to 2½″ long,
it is **KENTUCKY COFFEE-TREE**
Gymnocladus dioicus →

If each leaf is a fern-like spray of hundreds of small asymmetrical leaflets, shaped like flattened pea pods, and the tree has no thorns,

it is **MIMOSA SILK TREE**
Albizia julibrissin

(center leaf)

If each leaflet is symmetrical, and the tree has some compound and some doubly-compound leaves, and the tree has large thorns, usually branched, (lacking in some horticultural varieties),

it is **HONEY LOCUST**
Gleditsia triacanthos
(lower right)

x⅙ to ⅛

x¼

x¼

If there is one tooth, (occasionally 2), at each side of the base of each leaflet,

it is **TREE OF HEAVEN**
Ailanthus altissima

If there are teeth continuously along the margins of the leaflet, (in some cases the basal sections of the leaflets are without teeth),

go below to

If the leaf has milky juice, and the base of the leaf is enlarged to a cone that encircles next year's bud, and the leaf stem and twig are hairy, and the tree is crooked, shrubby, not tree-shaped,

it is **STAGHORN SUMAC**
Rhus typhina

If there is no milky juice and the tree is tree-shaped,

go on next page to

×¼

×¼

If all the leaflets are small, (not more than 1½″), on a small leaf, (usually not more than 6″ to 7″), on a small tree with clusters of white flowers or showy fruit,

go below to

If the leaflets are large, (usually 1½″ to 8″ long), on large leaves, (usually 8″ or more), and there is some evidence of nuts on or under the tree,

go on next page to

If the leaflets have somewhat blunted tips and are hairy beneath,

it is **EUROPEAN MOUNTAIN-ASH**
 Sorbus aucuparia

If the leaflets have pointed tips and are hairless,

it is **AMERICAN MOUNTAIN-ASH**
 Sorbus americana

If the crushed leaf is aromatic, and the end leaflet, if present, does not narrow gradually to an elongated, straight-sided V-base, and a long section of the twig reveals layered pith, and the husks of the nuts do not separate into sections,

go below to

If the end leaflet narrows gradually to a long, straight-sided V-shape, and the 3 end leaflets are usually distinctly larger than the basal leaflets, and the husks of the nuts separate,

go on next page to

If the end leaflet is small or lacking, and the side leaflets all taper continuously so that the sides are not parallel at any point,

it is **BLACK WALNUT** →
Juglans nigra

If the end leaflet is present, and if the sides of some of the leaflets are parallel along the mid-section,

it is **BUTTERNUT**
WHITE WALNUT
Juglans cinerea

$x\frac{1}{4}$ $x\frac{1}{4}$

If the leaflets at the tip of the leaf are much larger than the others, and if the leaf has only 5 to 7 leaflets, go below to

If the 3 tip leaflets are not much larger than the others, and the leaf has 7 to 11 leaflets,   go below to

If the underside of the leaves, and the stems and twigs, are covered with a dense, matted wool,

it is **MOCKERNUT HICKORY**
Carya tomentosa

If leaves and stem are smooth, and buds are yellow or have yellow hairs,

go on next page to

If the leaf is 6″ to 12″ long, and the twig is slender without an especially big end bud,   it is **PIGNUT HICKORY**
Carya glabra

If the leaf is 12″ to 20″ long, and the twigs are thick, with very big end buds,
it is **SHAGBARK HICKORY**
Carya ovata

If the leaf is small, (usually less than 12″), and the leaflets, (usually 7), are slightly hairy beneath, and the buds are mustard yellow,

it is **BITTERNUT HICKORY**
Carya cordiformis

If the leaf is 12″ to 20″ long, with 9 to 17 leaflets, and the buds have yellow hairs,

it is **PECAN**
Carya illinoensis

If the leaf has neither teeth nor lobes,

go on next page to

If the leaf has teeth of any kind, or a wavy margin, or lobes,

go on page 33 to

If the leaf is tipped with a single bristle (like the tip of a needle),

go below to

If the leaf has no bristle at its tip, (the leaf may be pointed or not),

go on next page to

If the leaf is dark green above and hairy beneath,

it is **SHINGLE OAK** →
Quercus imbricaria

If the leaf is light green above and veiny beneath, with a yellow midrib, and is ¼" to 1" wide,

it is **WILLOW OAK**
Quercus Phellos

x1-½   x1-½

If the leaf is heart-shaped, with veins branching from the base, it is **REDBUD**
Cercis canadensis

If the leaf is not heart-shaped,
go below to

If the leaf widens toward the base, and the veins are much branched, on a thorny, small tree, it is **OSAGE ORANGE**
Maclura pomifera

If the leaf is widest toward the tip, or toward the middle,
go below to

If all the leaves are unlobed,
go on next page to

If some of the leaves on the tree have no lobes but some are lobed,
go below to

If the leaves are thin and the bark and leaves are aromatic, and there are 3 forms of leaves,
it is **SASSAFRAS**
Sassafras albidum

If the leaves are thick, almost evergreen, and of several forms,
it is **WATER OAK**
Quercus nigra

If the leaves are only 2″ to 5″ long, thick, and shiny,   go below to

If the leaves are 5″ to 20″,   go below to

If the leaf is evergreen, with thickened in-rolled edges, dark green and lustrous above, and silvery-white and hairy below,   it is **LIVE OAK**
Quercus virginiana

If the leaf is deciduous, net-veined, with slender stem,   go below to

If the leaf is widest near the tip end and has a broad, flat midrib, it is **SOUR GUM or TUPELO**
Nyssa sylvatica

If the leaf is widest at the middle, with conspicuous, netted veins, curving with the undulating margin,   it is **PERSIMMON**
Diospyros virginiana

If there is a line, or scar, completely encircling the twig at each leaf, and the end buds are large,   go on next page to

If there is no line, and the buds are woolly, without scales, and the leaf stems are very short,   it is **PAWPAW** *Asimina triloba*

(31)

$\times \frac{1}{2}$

$\times \frac{1}{2}$

$\times \frac{1}{4}$

$\times \frac{1}{2}$

(32) If the leaves are evergreen, thick, leathery, rusty-hairy beneath,

it is **SOUTHERN MAGNOLIA** →
Magnolia grandiflora

If the leaves are deciduous and thin,

go below to

If the leaves are only 6″ to 10″, with silky-hairy end buds,

go below to

If the leaves are 10″ to 35″ long, and wider toward the tip,

go on next page to

If the leaf is oval, thin,

it is **CUCUMBER MAGNOLIA**
Magnolia acuminata

If the leaf is widest near the tip end, with an abruptly-tapering tip,

it is **SAUCER MAGNOLIA**
Magnolia soulangeana

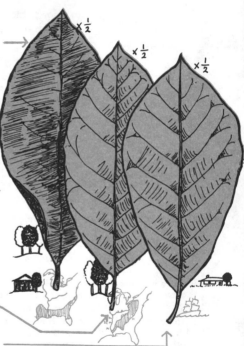

If the base of the leaf is heart-shaped, or ear-lobed,

go below to

If the base of the leaf is tapered,

it is **UMBRELLA MAGNOLIA** ⟶
Magnolia tripetala

If the base of the leaf is deeply ear-lobed, and the leaf is 8″ to 18″ long,

it is **MOUNTAIN MAGNOLIA**
Magnolia Fraseri
Center leaf

If the base is heart-shaped, and the leaf is whitish-hairy beneath, 12″ to 36″,

it is **LARGE-LEAVED MAGNOLIA**
Magnolia macrophylla
Right hand leaf

If the leaf is evergreen, tipped with stiff, sharp spines,

go on next page to

If the leaf is not evergreen,

go on next page to

(34)

If the surface of the leaf is dull, and the edge is not wavy,   it is **AMERICAN HOLLY**
Ilex opaca

If the surface of the leaf is glossy, and the edge is wavy,   it is **ENGLISH HOLLY**
Ilex aquifolium

If the tree has thorns or thorn-like twigs, and is small,
    go on page 46 to

If the tree has no thorns or thorn-like twigs,
    go below to

If the margin is toothed, or doubly-toothed continuously along all or almost all of its margin,
    go below to

If the leaf is either deeply or shallowly lobed or waved, (but not continuously saw-toothed),
    go on page 51 to

If the leaf is lobed as well as saw toothed, and is about as long as wide, with 3 to 5 main veins,
    go on page 54 to

If the leaf is not lobed,
    go on next page to

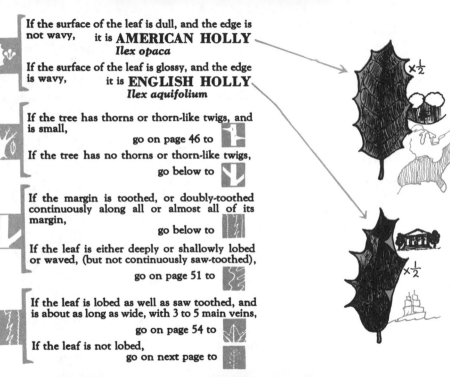

x ½

x ½

If the teeth are all of about the same size, go below to

If the margin is doubly-toothed, with small teeth between the larger ones, or with slightly deeper notches regularly spaced between teeth, go on page 45 to

If the teeth are of the same number as the side veins and terminate them, go below to

If teeth are more numerous than side veins and do not terminate them, go on page 37 to

If the leaf is 5″ to 8″ long, with teeth curving toward the tip of the leaf, go on next page to

If the leaf is thin, (2½″ to 5″ long), with shallow teeth, go below to

If the leaf is 2″ to 4″ long, not twice as long as wide, with inconspicuous teeth; and there are only 5 to 9 pairs of veins,

it is **EUROPEAN BEECH**
Fagus sylvatica

A variety with bronze-purple leaves, is **COPPER BEECH**
Fagus sylvatica purpurea

If the leaf is 3″ to 5″ long, more than twice as long as it is wide, and the teeth are more conspicuous; and there are 9 to 14 pairs of veins, it is

AMERICAN BEECH
Fagus grandifolia

x ½

x ½

BEECHES

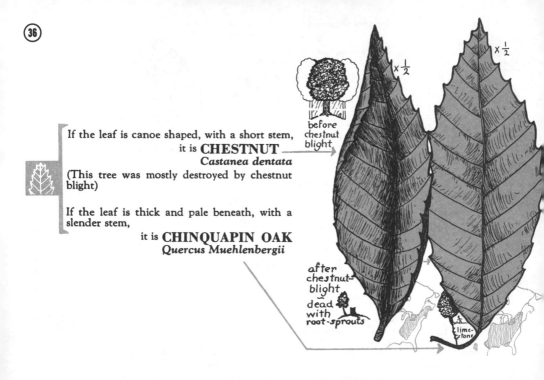

(36)

If the leaf is canoe shaped, with a short stem,
it is **CHESTNUT**
Castanea dentata

(This tree was mostly destroyed by chestnut blight)

If the leaf is thick and pale beneath, with a slender stem,

it is **CHINQUAPIN OAK**
Quercus Muehlenbergii

X ½

X ½

before chestnut blight

after chestnut-blight
dead with root-sprouts

lime-stone

If the leaf stem is long, (at least half as long as the blade), and the teeth are somewhat blunted, and the blade is wide, with firm texture and meshed veinlets, go below to

If the leaf does not have this combination of characteristics, go on page 40 to

If the stem of the leaf is flattened, go below to

If the stem of the leaf is not flattened, go on page 39 to

If the leaf blade is triangular, flat at the base, go below to

If the leaf base is rounded, go on page 38 to

If there are no glands on the leaf-stalk; the leaf has a translucent border and is finely-toothed; (12 or more teeth to an inch), and the tree is shaped like an exclamation point,

it is **LOMBARDY POPLAR**
Populus nigra variety *italica*

If the leaf stalk has 2 or 3 glands at the base of the blade, and the teeth are coarser, (about 5 to 8 to an inch), go on next page to

If the buds are sticky, and the leaf has a wide mid-vein,

it is **EASTERN COTTONWOOD**
Populus deltoides
figure on page 37, bottom

If the buds are slightly hairy, the mid-vein is narrow and the leaf narrows suddenly to a long, tapering tip,

it is **PLAINS COTTONWOOD**
Populus deltoides occidentalis
figure on page 37, right

If the leaf is not longer than it is broad, and the teeth are many and fine,

it is **TREMBLING ASPEN**
Populus tremuloides

If the leaf is longer than broad, with teeth coarse and few,

it is **BIG-TOOTHED ASPEN**
Populus grandidentata

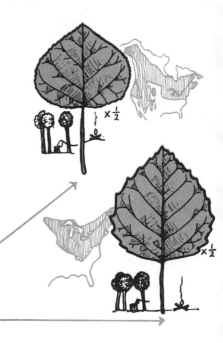

If the leaf has a rounded, or only slightly pointed tip; and a heart-shaped base; and is hairy, (sometimes only when newly unfolded),

it is **SWAMP COTTONWOOD** →
Populus heterophylla

If the leaf has a pointed tip, and fragrant buds,

go below to

If the leaf is oval, with a rounded base, and a smooth, slender stem and twigs,

it is **BALSAM POPLAR** ──────
Populus balsamifera

If the leaf is heart-shaped, and hairy on the under-surface, stem and twigs,

it is **BALM OF GILEAD** →
Populus gileadensis
(of unknown origin)

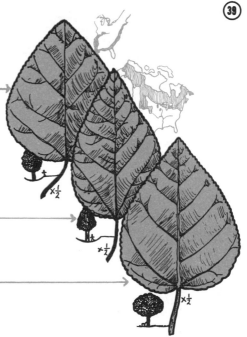

If the two side veins starting from the base of the blade are longer and more conspicuous than the other side veins,

go below to

If the side veins are all of about equal importance,

go on page 41 to

If the base of the leaf is definitely not symmetrical,

go below to

If the base is symmetrical, or only slightly asymmetrical, and the juice is milky, and some leaves are lobed, others unlobed,

go on next page to

If the leaf is broad,

go on next page to

If the leaf is narrow, long-pointed with a short stem, and no teeth at the base,

it is **HACKBERRY**
Celtis occidentalis

$\times \frac{1}{2}$

lime-
stone

If the leaf is hairless, it is **LINDEN AMERICAN BASSWOOD**
Tilia americana

If the underside of the leaf is velvety-white,
it is **WHITE BASSWOOD**
(upper right) *Tilia heterophylla*

If the leaf is rough above and hairy beneath, sometimes 2 or 3 lobed,
it is **RED MULBERRY**
Morus rubra

If the leaves are smooth above and not hairy beneath, usually lobed,
it is **WHITE MULBERRY**
(lower right) *Morus alba*

If the leaves are long and narrow, many-veined, tapering gradually and steadily to a long point, and the twigs are slender and limber, with only one scale covering each bud,

go on next page to

If the leaves and twigs are not thus, and the buds have more than one scale,

go on page 43 to

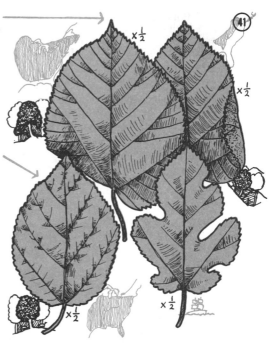

(42)

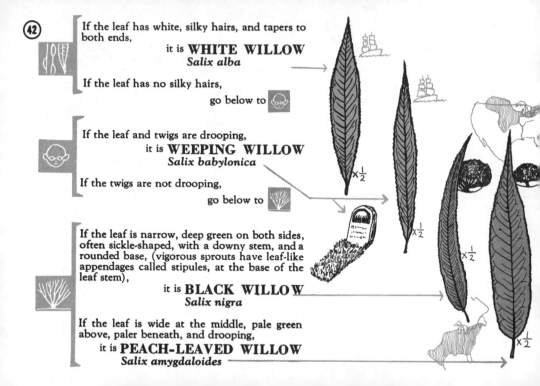

If the leaf has white, silky hairs, and tapers to both ends,

it is **WHITE WILLOW**
Salix alba

If the leaf has no silky hairs,

go below to

If the leaf and twigs are drooping,
it is **WEEPING WILLOW**
Salix babylonica

If the twigs are not drooping,

go below to

If the leaf is narrow, deep green on both sides, often sickle-shaped, with a downy stem, and a rounded base, (vigorous sprouts have leaf-like appendages called stipules, at the base of the leaf stem),

it is **BLACK WILLOW**
Salix nigra

If the leaf is wide at the middle, pale green above, paler beneath, and drooping,
it is **PEACH-LEAVED WILLOW**
Salix amygdaloides

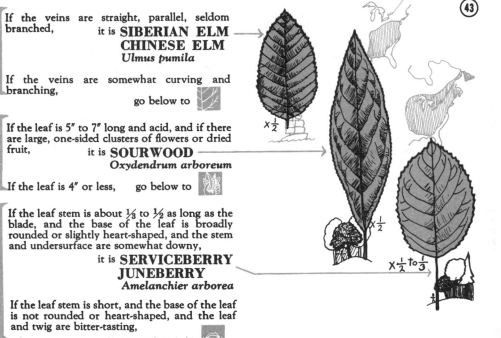

If the veins are straight, parallel, seldom branched, it is **SIBERIAN ELM CHINESE ELM** *Ulmus pumila*

If the veins are somewhat curving and branching, go below to

If the leaf is 5″ to 7″ long and acid, and if there are large, one-sided clusters of flowers or dried fruit, it is **SOURWOOD** *Oxydendrum arboreum*

If the leaf is 4″ or less, go below to

If the leaf stem is about ⅓ to ½ as long as the blade, and the base of the leaf is broadly rounded or slightly heart-shaped, and the stem and undersurface are somewhat downy, it is **SERVICEBERRY JUNEBERRY** *Amelanchier arborea*

If the leaf stem is short, and the base of the leaf is not rounded or heart-shaped, and the leaf and twig are bitter-tasting,

 go on next page to

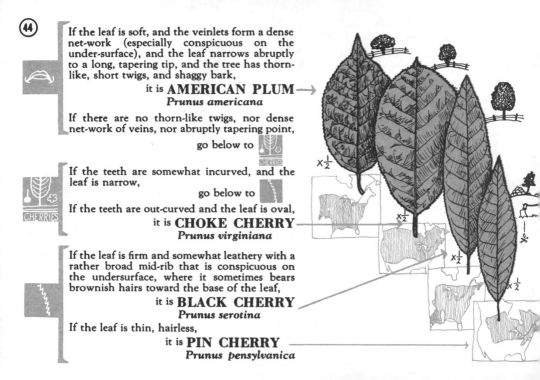

If the leaf is soft, and the veinlets form a dense net-work (especially conspicuous on the under-surface), and the leaf narrows abruptly to a long, tapering tip, and the tree has thorn-like, short twigs, and shaggy bark,

it is **AMERICAN PLUM** →
Prunus americana

If there are no thorn-like twigs, nor dense net-work of veins, nor abruptly tapering point,

go below to

If the teeth are somewhat incurved, and the leaf is narrow,

go below to

If the teeth are out-curved and the leaf is oval,

it is **CHOKE CHERRY** ——
Prunus virginiana

If the leaf is firm and somewhat leathery with a rather broad mid-rib that is conspicuous on the undersurface, where it sometimes bears brownish hairs toward the base of the leaf,

it is **BLACK CHERRY**
Prunus serotina

If the leaf is thin, hairless,

it is **PIN CHERRY** ——
Prunus pensylvanica

If the base of the leaf is lop-sided,

go below to

If the base of the leaf is symmetrical,

go on page 49 to

If the leaf is rough beneath, as well as on the upper surface, and if a flake of bark shows layers of red,

it is **SLIPPERY ELM** →
Ulmus rubra

If the leaf is not rough beneath,

go below to

If the leaf base is only slightly lop-sided, and there are usually some twigs with corky wings,

it is **CORK ELM**
Ulmus Thomasi

If the leaf is distinctly lop-sided, and either sand-paper-like or smooth above,

it is **AMERICAN ELM** →
Ulmus americana

(45)

If the thorns are smooth, tapering, often more than an inch long,

go below to

If the thorns are like stunted, pointed twigs, or stubby, blunt spurs,

go on page 48 to

If the leaves are widest at the base,

go below to

If the leaves taper to the base,

go on next page to

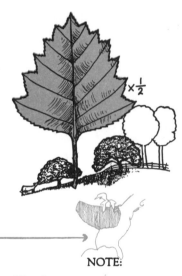

$\times \frac{1}{2}$

If the triangular leaf is hairy, soft, with a thick, hairy stem,

it is **DOWNY HAWTHORN**
Crataegus mollis

If the triangular leaf is smooth with a slender, smooth stem,

go on next page to

NOTE:

Hawthorns are too numerous to cover completely, these are the common ones.

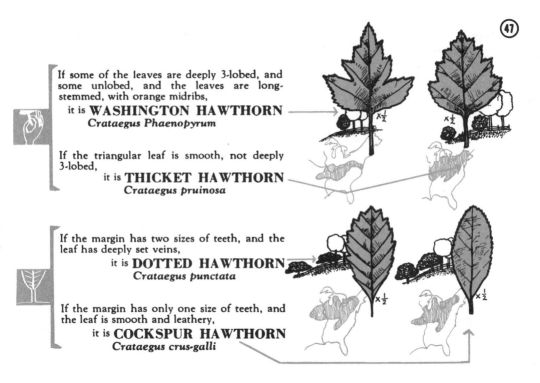

If some of the leaves are deeply 3-lobed, and some unlobed, and the leaves are long-stemmed, with orange midribs,

it is **WASHINGTON HAWTHORN**
Crataegus Phaenopyrum

If the triangular leaf is smooth, not deeply 3-lobed,

it is **THICKET HAWTHORN**
Crataegus pruinosa

If the margin has two sizes of teeth, and the leaf has deeply set veins,

it is **DOTTED HAWTHORN**
Crataegus punctata

If the margin has only one size of teeth, and the leaf is smooth and leathery,

it is **COCKSPUR HAWTHORN**
Crataegus crus-galli

47

(48)

If the leaf is not lobed, go below to

If the leaf is usually somewhat lobed, go below to

If twigs, leaf stems, and undersurfaces are woolly, it is **PRAIRIE CRABAPPLE** *Malus ioensis*

If the leaves and twigs are not woolly, it is **WILD CRABAPPLE** *Malus coronaria*

If the leaf surface, especially the undersurface, shows an intricate network of veins, and the leaf has a long, tapering tip, and the spurs are slender, it is **AMERICAN PLUM** see illustration page 44 *Prunus americana*

If the surface shows no intricate network, and the spurs are stout, go below to

If there is soft, woolly hair on the new shoots, and on the underside of the leaves, and on the leaf stems, and the spurs are seldom sharp-tipped, it is **COMMON APPLE** *Malus sylvestris*

If the leaf surfaces are smooth, and the margins have rounded teeth, and the spurs are usually sharp-tipped, it is **COMMON PEAR** *Pyrus communis*

$\times\frac{1}{2}$

$\times\frac{1}{2}$

$\times\frac{1}{2}$

$\times\frac{1}{2}$

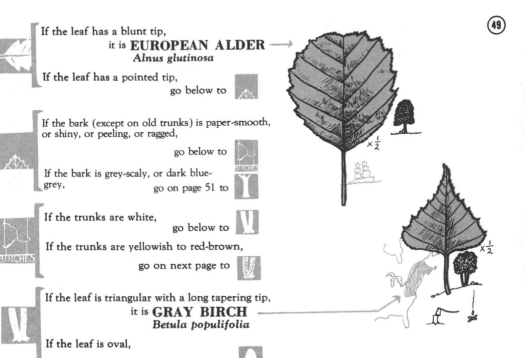

If the leaf has a blunt tip,
it is **EUROPEAN ALDER** →
Alnus glutinosa

If the leaf has a pointed tip,
go below to

If the bark (except on old trunks) is paper-smooth,
or shiny, or peeling, or ragged,
go below to

If the bark is grey-scaly, or dark blue-grey,
go on page 51 to

If the trunks are white,
go below to

If the trunks are yellowish to red-brown,
go on next page to

If the leaf is triangular with a long tapering tip,
it is **GRAY BIRCH** →
Betula populifolia

If the leaf is oval,
go on next page to

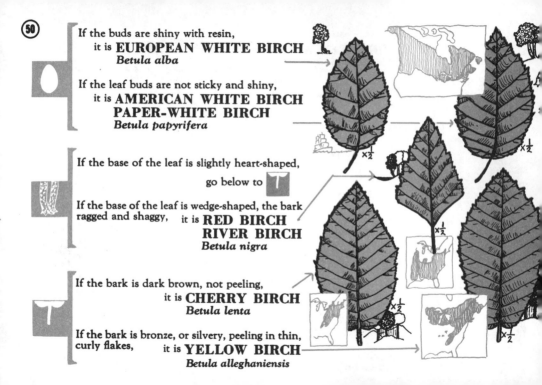

50

If the buds are shiny with resin,
it is **EUROPEAN WHITE BIRCH**
Betula alba

If the leaf buds are not sticky and shiny,
it is **AMERICAN WHITE BIRCH**
PAPER-WHITE BIRCH
Betula papyrifera

If the base of the leaf is slightly heart-shaped,
go below to

If the base of the leaf is wedge-shaped, the bark
ragged and shaggy, it is **RED BIRCH**
RIVER BIRCH
Betula nigra

If the bark is dark brown, not peeling,
it is **CHERRY BIRCH**
Betula lenta

If the bark is bronze, or silvery, peeling in thin,
curly flakes, it is **YELLOW BIRCH**
Betula alleghaniensis

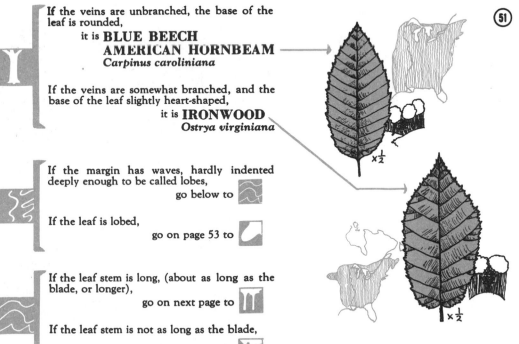

If the veins are unbranched, the base of the leaf is rounded,

it is **BLUE BEECH**
AMERICAN HORNBEAM —⟶
Carpinus caroliniana

If the veins are somewhat branched, and the base of the leaf slightly heart-shaped,

it is **IRONWOOD**
Ostrya virginiana

If the margin has waves, hardly indented deeply enough to be called lobes,

go below to

If the leaf is lobed,

go on page 53 to

If the leaf stem is long, (about as long as the blade, or longer),

go on next page to

If the leaf stem is not as long as the blade,

go on next page to

x ½

x ½

If the leaf has a felt-like, white undersurface, (some of the leaves may be lobed),

it is **WHITE POPLAR**
Populus alba

If the veins are arranged like the ribs of a fan,

it is **GINKGO**
Figure page 54   *Ginkgo biloba*

If the leaf is usually bristle-tipped, and widest at the tip, and some leaves on the tree are lobed,

go below to

If there are no bristle tips,

go on next page to

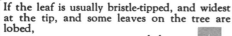

If the leaves are small, 2″ to 4″, shining on both sides, almost evergreen, and there may be both lobed and unlobed leaves, and wavy-edged leaves, and leaves with and without bristles, all on the same tree,   it is **WATER OAK**
Quercus nigra

If the leaves are 4″ to 6″ long, usually with bristles on the 3 to 5 waves or lobes, (sometimes without bristles), and the underside is rusty-hairy,

it is **BLACKJACK OAK**
Quercus marilandica

If the waves are regular, and rounded, and the leaves are broadly oval,

it is **CHESTNUT OAK**
Quercus Prinus
(left leaf)

If the waves are irregular, sometimes almost deep enough to be called lobes, and the leaves are soft and hairy beneath,

it is **SWAMP-WHITE OAK**
Quercus bicolor
(right leaf)

If the leaf has only 2, 3 or 4 lobes,

go on next page to

If the leaf has more than 4 lobes,

go on page 55 to

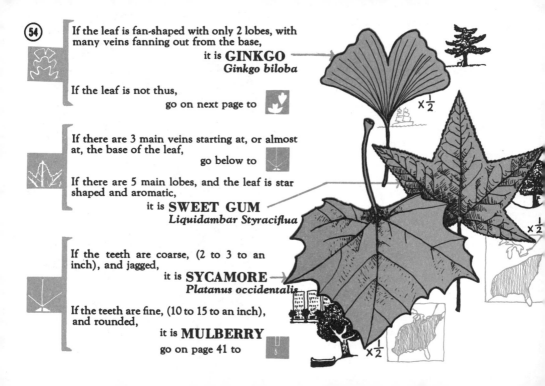

(54)

If the leaf is fan-shaped with only 2 lobes, with many veins fanning out from the base,

it is **GINKGO**
Ginkgo biloba

If the leaf is not thus,

go on next page to

If there are 3 main veins starting at, or almost at, the base of the leaf,

go below to

If there are 5 main lobes, and the leaf is star shaped and aromatic,

it is **SWEET GUM**
Liquidambar Styraciflua

If the teeth are coarse, (2 to 3 to an inch), and jagged,

it is **SYCAMORE**
Platanus occidentalis

If the teeth are fine, (10 to 15 to an inch), and rounded,

it is **MULBERRY**
go on page 41 to

If the tree has some lobed leaves and some unlobed leaves,
go below to

If the main vein ends in a notch, and the tip looks cut off, it is **TULIP TREE**
Liriodendron Tulipifera
right-hand leaf

If the leaf is thin and some leaves are mitten-shaped, it is **SASSAFRAS**
Sassafras albidum
left-hand leaf

If the leaf is thick and leathery,
go on page 52 to

If the lobes are bristle-pointed,
go below to

If the lobes are rounded,
go on page 58 to

If the leaf is not deeply lobed, (not more than half-way to the mid-rib),
go on next page to

If the leaf is deeply lobed, (more than half-way to the mid-rib),
go on next page to

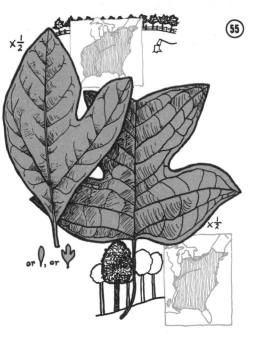

×½   ×½

or ⸙, or

(56)

If the leaf is small, white-downy beneath on a small tree,
it is **SCRUB OAK**
BEAR OAK
Quercus ilicifolia →

If the leaf is not thus,
go below to

If the tip end of the leaf is narrow, long, (about ⅓ to ½ the length of the blade),
it is **SPANISH OAK**
Quercus falcata
(lower right leaf)

If the leaf is not thus,
go on page 57 to

If the leaf is thin, firm, smooth beneath, 5″ to 9″ long, with lobes that taper toward their tips, usually more than 7-lobed,
it is **RED OAK**
Quercus rubra

If the leaf is thick, leathery, usually widening toward the tip, usually 7-lobed, somewhat hairy beneath, (the tree usually has several different forms of leaves), and the buds are angled,
it is **BLACK OAK**
Quercus velutina
(upper right leaves)

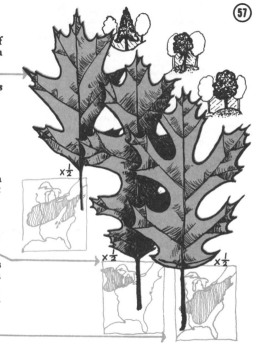

If the lobes taper toward their tips and the leaf is small, (3″ to 4″), often only 5-lobed, with a wedge-shaped base,

it is **PIN OAK** ◀
Quercus palustris

If the lobes broaden toward their tips,

go below to

If the leaf is dark green, shining, oval, on an untidy-looking tree, usually with the lowest branches dead,

it is **HILL'S OAK**
JACK OAK
Quercus ellipsoidalis

If the leaf is thin, delicate, with lobes sometimes almost enclosing oval spaces, and with a yellow mid-rib,

it is **SCARLET OAK**
Quercus coccinea

x½   x½   x½

(58)

If the leaf is small, (2″ to 4″), and has ear-like lobes at the base, and a *very* short stem,

it is **ENGLISH OAK**
Quercus Robur
(lower right leaf)

If the leaf is not thus,
go below to

If the lobes are square cut, with the 3 end lobes much larger than the others, it is **POST OAK**
Quercus stellata
(lower left leaf)

If the lobes are not thus,
go below to

If the lobes are somewhat similar in size and shape,

it is **WHITE OAK**
Quercus alba
(upper left leaf)

If the middle of the leaf is cut nearly to the midrib, on most of the leaves, and the upper half of the leaf is not deeply lobed,

it is **BUR OAK**
Quercus macrocarpa
(upper right leaf)

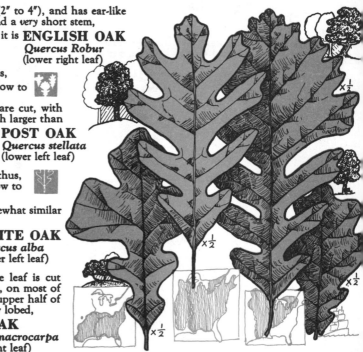

Other books in the pocket-sized "finder" series:

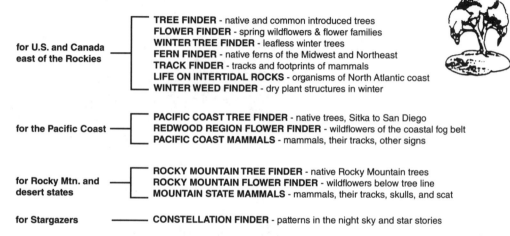

for U.S. and Canada east of the Rockies
- **TREE FINDER** - native and common introduced trees
- **FLOWER FINDER** - spring wildflowers & flower families
- **WINTER TREE FINDER** - leafless winter trees
- **FERN FINDER** - native ferns of the Midwest and Northeast
- **TRACK FINDER** - tracks and footprints of mammals
- **LIFE ON INTERTIDAL ROCKS** - organisms of North Atlantic coast
- **WINTER WEED FINDER** - dry plant structures in winter

for the Pacific Coast
- **PACIFIC COAST TREE FINDER** - native trees, Sitka to San Diego
- **REDWOOD REGION FLOWER FINDER** - wildflowers of the coastal fog belt
- **PACIFIC COAST MAMMALS** - mammals, their tracks, other signs

for Rocky Mtn. and desert states
- **ROCKY MOUNTAIN TREE FINDER** - native Rocky Mountain trees
- **ROCKY MOUNTAIN FLOWER FINDER** - wildflowers below tree line
- **MOUNTAIN STATE MAMMALS** - mammals, their tracks, skulls, and scat

for Stargazers
- **CONSTELLATION FINDER** - patterns in the night sky and star stories

NATURE STUDY GUIDES are published by KEEN COMMUNICATIONS, PO Box 43673, Birmingham, AL 35243 (888) 604-4537, naturestudy.com. SEE keencommunication.com for our full line of outdoor activity guides by MENASHA RIDGE PRESS and WILDERNESS PRESS. Including regional and national parks hiking, camping, backpacking, and more.